HORS D'OEUVRES AND APPETIZERS

Caroline Ellwood

🦁 GOLDEN PRESS / NEW YORK
Western Publishing Company, Inc.
Racine, Wisconsin

CONTENTS

NOTES:

Always preheat the oven to the specified temperature.

Margarine can be substituted for butter in all recipes.

If substituting dried herbs for fresh, use a third of the amount;
if substituting fresh for dried, use 3 times the amount.

This edition prepared under the supervision of
Joanna Morris

This edition published 1984 by Golden Press
Library of Congress Catalog Card Number: 84-80339
ISBN 0-307-09964-4
Golden® and Golden Press® are registered trademarks
of Western Publishing Company, Inc.

First published in the U.K. by Cathay Books,
59 Grosvenor Street, London W1

INTRODUCTION

Whether you're looking for a variety of tidbits to serve along with drinks or a special starter course for an all-important dinner party, you're sure to find a wealth of ideas on the following pages.

There are dips and spreads in abundance, as well as a host of finger foods, both hot and cold. For sit-down appetizers, you can choose from a wide selection of unusual fruit and vegetable combinations, flaky filled tarts and quiches, delicate crepes and seafood starters. There's even a whole section devoted to pâtés, terrines and mousses.

When choosing a dish for a first course, the intent is to set the stage for the food to come. You want to whet the appetite, not kill it. When it comes to stand-up party fare, the rule is variety. Serve both hot and cold, crunchy and smooth, light and hearty. For the ease and comfort of your guests, remember to have stacks of little plates at hand as well as plenty of cocktail napkins.

With recipes like these, your parties will always be off to a good start.

HORS D'OEUVRES

Sardine Dip

2 cans (3¾ oz each)
    sardines in oil,
    drained
½ package (8 oz size)
    cream cheese,
    softened
2 tablespoons lemon
    juice
4 parsley sprigs
⅓ cup sour cream

Place the sardines, cream cheese, lemon juice, parsley sprigs and sour cream in blender container; blend at high speed 30 seconds.

Spoon dip into a small serving bowl. Serve with rye toast.

About 1 cup

Smoked Whitefish Spread

12 oz boneless
  smoked whitefish,
  skin removed
½ package (8 oz size)
  cream cheese,
  softened
2 tablespoons butter,
  melted
4 tablespoons
  half-and-half
1 teaspoon lemon
  juice
½ teaspoon dried dill
  weed
Salt and pepper

Cut one third of the fish into finger-length pieces; reserve. Place the remaining fish, the cream cheese, butter, half-and-half, lemon juice and dill weed in blender container or food processor fitted with steel blade; blend until smooth, scraping down the side of container as necessary. Add salt and pepper to taste.

Spoon half of the fish mixture into a small terrine or crock. Arrange the fish pieces on top. Cover with the remaining fish mixture and smooth the top. Refrigerate until serving time. Serve with toast.

About 2 cups

Eggplant Dip

2 medium eggplant
1 clove garlic, chopped
1 tablespoon red wine vinegar
1 tablespoon olive oil
Salt and pepper
2 tomatoes, seeded and finely chopped
1 small onion, finely chopped

Prick eggplant all over with a fork; cut in half. Place cut side down on a greased baking sheet. Bake in a preheated 375° oven until soft, 30 to 40 minutes. Peel and cut into chunks.

Place eggplant, garlic, vinegar, oil and salt and pepper to taste in a blender; blend at high speed until smooth, about 1 minute. Stir in the tomatoes and onion.

To serve attractively, line a serving dish with lettuce leaves. Spoon on the eggplant dip. Garnish with tomato slices, onion rings and olives. Accompany with sliced French bread or a variety of crackers.
About 2½ cups

Hummus

1 can (15 oz) chick peas
2 tablespoons tahine
2 cloves garlic, chopped
Grated rind and juice of ½ lemon
3 tablespoons olive oil
Salt and pepper

Drain the chick peas, reserving the liquid. Place the chick peas, tahine, garlic, lemon rind and juice and olive oil in a blender and puree, scraping down the sides of the container as necessary. Add reserved liquid if necessary for dipping consistency. Add salt and pepper to taste. Spoon into a bowl; sprinkle with chopped parsley if desired.
About 2 cups

NOTE: Tahine is a sesame seed paste. It is available in most supermarkets and health food stores.

Taramasalata

3 oz tarama
3 slices bread, crusts removed, cut into cubes
2 tablespoons water
Juice of 1 small lemon
1 clove garlic, chopped
4 tablespoons olive oil

Place tarama, bread, water, lemon juice and garlic in a blender container; puree at low speed 30 seconds, scraping the sides of the container as necessary. With blender on medium speed, pour in olive oil 1 teaspoon at a time, blending until thick. Spoon into a small bowl. Serve with crusty bread and lemon wedges.

About 1 cup

NOTE: Tarama is codfish roe. It is available in jars in supermarkets and specialty food shops.

9

Potted Chicken and Ham

¾ cup butter, melted
1 cup chopped
  cooked chicken
¼ cup chopped ham
Pinch of grated
  nutmeg
Salt and pepper

Skim the froth from the melted butter and spoon off 4 tablespoons clear butter; reserve. Place half the chicken and ham, 4 tablespoons of the remaining butter and the nutmeg in a blender; puree. Transfer the mixture to a small bowl.

Repeat with the remaining chicken and ham and 4 tablespoons butter; combine the mixtures in a bowl and season to taste with salt and pepper.

Press the mixture into a small serving dish with the back of a spoon; smooth the surface. Pour the reserved clear butter over the surface to coat completely. Cover with plastic wrap and refrigerate until set.

About 1½ cups

NOTE: This will keep in the refrigerator up to 4 days. The layer of clarified butter acts as a preservative.

Herbed Chicken Liver Mold

2 tablespoons oil
1 medium onion, chopped
8 oz chicken livers
1 clove garlic, chopped
1 tablespoon chopped parsley
¾ teaspoon each dried thyme and marjoram
¾ cup butter, melted
1 tablespoon brandy
Salt and pepper

Heat the oil in a medium skillet. Cook the onion just until softened. Add the chicken livers, garlic, parsley and herbs. Cook over high heat until the livers are cooked but still pink inside, 3 to 5 minutes. Cool slightly. Cut livers into pieces.

Skim the melted butter of froth and spoon off 4 tablespoons clear butter; reserve. Place the liver mixture, ½ cup melted butter and brandy in a blender; puree. Transfer to a bowl and season to taste with salt and pepper; let cool. Beat with a fork until fluffy and smooth.

Spoon into a small serving dish and smooth the surface. Pour the reserved clear butter over the surface. Refrigerate until set.

About 1½ cups

11

Elegant Cheese Mold

8 oz small-curd
  cottage cheese
2 teaspoons minced
  onion
2 tomatoes, peeled,
  seeded and finely
  chopped
1 tablespoon
  anchovy paste
Worcestershire
  sauce
Salt and pepper

Mix the cheese, onion, tomatoes, anchovy paste and Worcestershire and salt and pepper to taste in a small bowl. Press the mixture into an oiled 1-cup mold or the cottage cheese carton. Refrigerate for 2 to 3 hours.

Unmold onto a serving dish. To serve attractively, arrange shredded lettuce around the mold and garnish with tomato slices and parsley.

About 2 cups

Variations:
1. Omit tomatoes, anchovy paste and Worcestershire. Add ¼ cup chopped walnuts.
2. Replace the anchovy paste and Worcestershire with 2 teaspoons each chopped parsley and chopped chives and 1 teaspoon dried thyme leaves.

Three-Cheese Spread

3 oz blue cheese
½ cup grated Swiss
  cheese
½ cup grated
  Cheddar cheese
2 tablespoons plain
  yogurt
4 tablespoons
  half-and-half
2 teaspoons chopped
  chives
2 teaspoons chopped
  parsley
¼ teaspoon Dijon
  mustard

Mash the blue cheese in a small bowl until softened; add the Swiss and Cheddar cheeses. Mix in remaining ingredients until well blended.

Spoon into a serving bowl. Cover and refrigerate overnight. Remove from refrigerator 1 hour before serving. Serve with pumpernickel or crackers.
About 1½ cups

NOTE: Other semi-firm cheeses, such as brick, Muenster, Jarlsberg, Emmenthal or Monterey Jack, can be substituted for the Swiss or Cheddar cheese.

Spicy Clam Dip

1 package (3 oz)
  cream cheese,
  softened
1 tablespoon milk
1 can (6½ oz) clams,
  drained
2 teaspoons chopped
  chives
2 green onions,
  minced
1 teaspoon lemon
  juice
½ teaspoon prepared
  horseradish with
  beets
3 drops
  Worcestershire
  sauce
Few dashes of hot
  pepper sauce
Salt and pepper

Beat the cheese with the milk in a small bowl until fluffy. Mix in the clams, chives, green onions, lemon juice, horseradish, Worcestershire and hot pepper sauce. Add salt and pepper to taste.

Spoon into a bowl and chill until serving time. Garnish with additional chopped chives. Serve with bread sticks or crackers.

About 1 cup

Deviled Ham Spread

1 cup minced cooked
  ham
½ cup finely
  chopped walnuts
½ cup grated
  Cheddar cheese
1 teaspoon cider
  vinegar
1 teaspoon Dijon
  mustard
½ cup mayonnaise
2 tablespoons sour
  cream

Mix the ham, walnuts and cheese in a small bowl. Stir in the vinegar and mustard until well mixed. Stir in the mayonnaise and sour cream.

Refrigerate until serving time. Garnish with a lemon slice.

About 1½ cups

NOTE: Chopped pecans can be substituted for the walnuts. If desired, spread nuts in a pan and toast in a 400° oven for 5 minutes before adding.

Boursin-Stuffed Eggs

4 hard-cooked eggs
2 oz Boursin or other
  semi-soft cheese
  with garlic
3 tablespoons
  half-and-half
2 tablespoons
  chopped walnuts
Salt and pepper
Paprika

Cut the eggs in half lengthwise; remove the yolks. Mash the yolks in a
small bowl with the cheese and cream;
mix well. Stir in the walnuts and salt
and pepper to taste. Spoon or pipe the
yolk mixture into egg whites. Garnish
with paprika.
8 hors d'oeuvres

15

Meatballs with Pepper Dip

½ cup sour cream
½ green pepper,
  finely chopped
½ sweet red pepper,
  finely chopped
1 clove garlic,
  minced
Dash of hot pepper
  sauce
Salt and pepper
½ lb ground beef
½ small onion,
  minced
1 egg, beaten
1½ tablespoons
  vegetable oil

Mix sour cream, peppers, garlic, hot pepper sauce and salt and pepper to taste in a small bowl. Set aside.

Mix the beef, onion and egg and season to taste with salt and pepper. Shape into small meatballs. Heat the oil in a medium skillet. Sauté the meatballs, a few at a time, until well browned. Drain on paper towels. Serve hot with pepper dip.

About 16 meatballs

Sherried Liver Spread

4 tablespoons butter
1 lb chicken livers
1 medium onion,
   chopped
1 clove garlic,
   crushed
1 tablespoon heavy
   cream
2 tablespoons
   tomato paste
3 tablespoons dry
   sherry
Salt and pepper

Melt the butter in a medium skillet. Add the chicken livers; cook over high heat until lightly browned, 2 to 3 minutes. Add the onion and garlic; cover and cook over low heat 5 minutes. Stir in the cream, tomato paste and sherry. Place the mixture in a blender and puree. Add salt and pepper to taste.

Spoon the spread into a 2-cup bowl; smooth the top. Refrigerate until thoroughly chilled. Garnish with parsley and serve with assorted crackers.
About 2 cups

17

Minted Lamb Meatballs

1 lb ground lamb
2 cloves garlic,
  minced
2 teaspoons mint
  jelly
¾ teaspoon salt
½ teaspoon pepper
1 egg, beaten
2 tablespoons oil
2 tablespoons
  packed brown
  sugar
2 teaspoons
  cornstarch
3 tablespoons water
4 tablespoons red
  currant jelly
2 tablespoons
  Worcestershire
  sauce

Mix the lamb, garlic, mint jelly, salt, pepper and egg in a bowl. Shape the mixture into walnut-size meatballs. Heat the oil in a medium skillet over medium heat. Sauté meatballs, one-fourth at a time, until golden brown on all sides. Drain on paper towels. Keep warm in the oven until ready to serve.

Place the sugar, cornstarch and water in a small saucepan. Stir in the currant jelly and Worcestershire. Heat to boiling over low heat, stirring constantly until the dip is smooth.

Serve warm meatballs with warm dip. Accompany with cocktail picks.
About 25 meatballs

18

Satay with Peanut Sauce

1 teaspoon chili
  powder
1 teaspoon water
1 tablespoon oil
1 onion, grated
1 clove garlic,
  minced
2 tablespoons lemon
  juice
5 tablespoons water
4 tablespoons
  chunky peanut
  butter
1 teaspoon salt
1 teaspoon each
  ground cumin and
  coriander
12 oz pork
  tenderloin

Mix the chili powder and water to make a paste. Heat the oil in a small saucepan over medium heat. Add the onion, garlic and chili paste; cook, stirring occasionally, until the onion is soft, about 5 minutes. Stir in the remaining ingredients except pork. Spoon into a serving bowl.

Cut the pork into ½-inch pieces. Thread onto long wooden picks, 3 or 4 pieces per pick. Place picks under a preheated broiler until the meat is cooked through, about 1 minute on each side. Serve warm, with peanut sauce. Garnish with lemon and parsley if desired.

About 20 skewers

Spicy Guacamole

2 avocados, peeled
 and pitted
1 onion, finely
 chopped
1 large tomato,
 chopped
1 to 2 tablespoons
 canned chopped
 jalapeño peppers
 with juice
2 tablespoons
 chopped coriander
1½ tablespoons lime
 juice

Mash the avocados with the onion in a bowl. Stir in the tomato, jalapeño peppers, 1 tablespoon of the coriander and the lime juice. Sprinkle with the remaining coriander. Serve with tortilla chips.

About 2 cups

Blue Cheese Dip

½ cup crumbled
 blue cheese
½ package (8-oz size)
 cream cheese
1 tablespoon port
2 tablespoons milk
2 sprigs parsley,
 stems removed

Combine all the ingredients in a blender and puree.

Spoon the dip into a serving bowl. Serve with an assortment of crackers or cut-up raw vegetables.

About 1 cup

Green Pepper Dip

2 packages (3 oz
 each) cream
 cheese
½ cup grated
 Cheddar cheese
2 tablespoons sour
 cream
1 clove garlic,
 crushed
1 green pepper,
 seeded and
 minced
Hot pepper sauce
Salt and pepper

Combine the cheeses, sour cream and garlic in a blender and puree until smooth. Stir in the green pepper and season to taste with hot pepper sauce, salt and pepper. Chill.

Serve with raw vegetable dippers.

About 2 cups

Walnut Dip

1 cup shelled
walnuts
1 clove garlic,
crushed
1 tablespoon olive
oil
1 teaspoon lemon
juice
1 cup plain yogurt
Salt and pepper
¼ cucumber, peeled

Place the walnuts, garlic, oil and lemon juice in a blender and puree. Add the yogurt and blend until smooth. Add salt and pepper to taste. Spoon into a serving bowl. Finely chop the cucumber and stir in. Chill until ready to serve.

About 2 cups

Creamy Avocado Dip

2 avocados
1½ tablespoons
lemon juice
2 tomatoes, chopped
2 cloves garlic,
minced
1 small onion, grated
1 package (3 oz)
cream cheese

Peel and pit the avocados. Mash with the lemon juice in a small mixer bowl. Beat in tomatoes, garlic, onion and cheese. Add salt and pepper if desired.

Spoon into a serving bowl. Serve with crackers.

About 1¼ cups

Tapenade

½ cup stuffed green
  olives
1 can (3½ oz) tuna,
  drained
1 can (2 oz)
  anchovies,
  drained
3 tablespoons capers
2 teaspoons lemon
  juice
½ cup olive oil
1 tablespoon brandy
Dijon mustard

Slice 2 or 3 of the olives and reserve for
garnish. Place the remaining olives,
the tuna, anchovies, capers, lemon
juice, oil and brandy in a blender and
puree. Stir in the mustard to taste.

Spoon into a serving bowl. Garnish
with the sliced olives. Serve with bread
or crackers.

About 2 cups

Roquefort Dill Dip

4 oz each Roquefort
  and cottage cheese
4 tablespoons plain
  yogurt
1 tablespoon minced
  parsley
1 teaspoon dill weed

Beat all ingredients in a bowl until
smooth. Spoon into a serving bowl.
Serve with crackers, celery sticks or
thin melon wedges.

About 1 cup

23

Barbecue Dip

3 green onions,
  minced
½ green pepper,
  finely chopped
1 cup grated sharp
  Cheddar cheese
⅔ cup plain yogurt
1 tablespoon catsup
1 tablespoon
  mayonnaise
½ teaspoon
  Worcestershire
  sauce
Few drops of hot
  pepper sauce
Salt and pepper

Combine all ingredients in a small bowl, adding salt and pepper to taste. Spoon into a serving bowl. Chill until ready to serve. Just before serving, sprinkle with paprika if desired, and serve with vegetable dippers.
About 2 cups

Fruity Cheese Dip

8 oz cottage cheese
  with pineapple
½ cup grated
  Cheddar cheese
¼ cup heavy cream,
  whipped
Finely grated rind of
  1 orange
8 green grapes,
  chopped
1 stalk celery,
  chopped
½ teaspoon celery
  salt
Salt and pepper

Mix the cheeses and cream in a small bowl. Stir in the orange rind, grapes, celery and celery salt. Add salt and pepper to taste.

Spoon into a serving bowl and garnish with parsley if desired. Serve with crackers or with sliced apples, pears, cucumbers or melon.

About 2 cups

Alpine Fondue

1 clove garlic, cut in
half
½ cup dry white
wine
1 teaspoon lemon
juice
6 oz Gruyère or
Swiss cheese,
grated
6 oz Emmenthal or
Swiss cheese,
grated
1 teaspoon
cornstarch
1 tablespoon
cherry-flavored
liqueur
Pepper
Nutmeg

Rub the inside of a fondue pot or heavy saucepan with the cut side of the garlic. Add the wine and lemon juice; heat until simmering. Reduce heat and stir in the cheeses gradually, stirring constantly until melted and beginning to simmer.

Blend the cornstarch and liqueur in a small bowl. Stir into the cheese mixture. Cook over low heat, stirring constantly, until the mixture is thick and creamy, 2 to 3 minutes. Add pepper and nutmeg to taste.

Serve with bread cubes for dippers.

About 2 cups

Cheddar Beer Fondue

½ small onion, cut
in half
1 cup beer
1 tablespoon lemon
juice
1 lb Cheddar cheese,
grated
1 tablespoon
cornstarch
2 tablespoons sherry
Pinch of dry mustard
1 teaspoon
Worcestershire
sauce
Pepper

Rub the inside of a fondue pot or heavy saucepan with the cut side of the onion. Add the beer and lemon juice; heat to boiling. Reduce heat and stir in the cheese gradually, stirring until melted and beginning to simmer.

Blend the cornstarch and sherry in a small bowl; stir in the mustard, Worcestershire and pepper to taste. Add to the cheese mixture. Cook over low heat, stirring constantly, until the mixture is thick and creamy, 2 to 3 minutes.

Serve with bread cubes for dippers.

About 3 cups

Skordalia Sauce with Vegetable Dippers

4 egg yolks
6 large cloves garlic, crushed
1 cup olive oil
½ cup ground almonds
1 cup fresh bread crumbs
2 tablespoons lemon juice
1 tablespoon chopped parsley

Place the egg yolks and garlic in a blender. Turn on high speed and add the olive oil very slowly, 1 teaspoon at a time, until the mixture begins to thicken; then very slowly pour in the remaining oil. Transfer the mixture to a serving bowl. Stir in the ground almonds, bread crumbs, lemon juice, and chopped parsley. Refrigerate until serving time.

Serve the sauce with a wide variety of dippers. Choose from among the following: blanched and chilled green beans, cauliflower flowerets, radishes, carrot and celery sticks, jicama slices, green onions, very thin zucchini and cucumber sticks, cherry tomatoes or thin wedges of tomato. Arrange the vegetables attractively on a round platter and center with the sauce.
About 2 cups

Blinis

¾ cup warm milk
1 package active
  dry yeast
1 teaspoon sugar
½ cup buckwheat
  flour
½ cup all-purpose
  flour
2 eggs, separated
1 jar (2 oz) lumpfish
  caviar
4 oz sliced smoked
  salmon
1 cup sour cream
3 green onions,
  chopped

Mix the milk, yeast and sugar; let stand 10 minutes. Sift the flours into a large bowl. Make a well in the center and pour in the milk mixture; gradually beat into the flour. Beat the egg yolks into the batter. Cover and let stand in a warm place for about 1 hour. Beat the egg whites until stiff peaks form and fold into the batter.

Drop a tablespoon of the batter at a time into a greased small skillet. Cook over medium heat until the blini is lightly browned on one side; turn and lightly brown the other side. Cover and keep warm.

To serve, spread half the blinis with caviar; top the remaining blinis with smoked salmon. Accompany with sour cream and green onions.

18 blinis

Open Sandwiches

Spread any of the suggested bases with butter. Season butter, if desired, with prepared mustard, herbs or Worcestershire sauce. Place a slice of one of the cheeses on top. Add a meat or seafood and one or more garnishes.

Bases:
French bread
Rye bread
Pumpernickel
  bread
Norwegian flat
  bread

Meat & Seafood:
Cold cuts
Pâté
Smoked turkey
Smoked salmon
Shrimp

Cheeses:
Cheddar
Swiss
Edam
Gouda
Port-Salut
Jarlsberg
Blue cheese
Muenster
Brick
Monterey Jack
Cream cheese
Havarti
Provolone

Garnishes:
Onion rings
Parsley
Cucumber
  twists
Watercress
Tomato slices
Sliced gherkins
Sliced olives
Hard-cooked
  eggs
Pepper rings
Shredded lettuce
Radish slices
Pineapple
  chunks
Orange slices

Cheese Straws

¾ cup all-purpose
  flour
Pinch of salt
Pinch of cayenne
  pepper
4 tablespoons butter
½ cup grated sharp
  Cheddar cheese
1 egg yolk
2 teaspoons ketchup
2 to 3 teaspoons
  water
1 egg, beaten
Paprika

Sift the flour, salt and cayenne pepper
into a medium bowl. Cut in the butter
until the mixture resembles coarse
crumbs. Stir in the cheese. Stir in the
egg yolk, ketchup and enough water to
make a stiff dough.

Roll out the dough to ¼-inch thickness on a lightly floured surface. Brush
with the beaten egg; sprinkle with paprika. Cut into ½-inch strips; cut the
strips to make 3-inch lengths.

Place the strips on a greased baking
sheet. Bake in the center of a preheated
400° oven until pale golden, 10 to 15
minutes. Cool on a wire rack.

About 25 straws

NOTE: Dough can also be cut into
rounds with a 1½-inch cutter. Bake as
directed above. If desired, spread with
softened cream cheese and sprinkle
with poppy seeds.

Spiced Almonds

3 tablespoons
   vegetable oil
1 cup slivered
   almonds
1 teaspoon salt
1 teaspoon curry
   powder

Heat the oil in a medium skillet. Add the almonds; sauté until golden brown. Drain on paper towels. Mix the salt and curry powder and sprinkle over the almonds, tossing to coat the nuts evenly.

1 cup

Cheese Crackers

¾ cup all-purpose
   flour
4 tablespoons butter
½ cup grated
   Cheddar cheese
1 egg yolk
2 teaspoons cold
   water

Sift the flour into a medium bowl. Cut in butter until the mixture resembles coarse crumbs. Stir in the cheese. Stir in the egg yolk and water to make a firm dough.

Turn the dough onto a lightly floured surface. Roll out to ¼-inch thickness. Cut into 1½-inch rounds with a plain cutter.

Place the crackers 1 inch apart on a greased baking sheet. Bake in a pre-heated 400° oven, 10 minutes. Cool on a wire rack. Serve plain or with dips and spreads.

About 50 crackers

Chive Crackers

½ cup butter
1½ packages (3 oz
   each) cream
   cheese
¾ cup all-purpose
   flour, sifted
¼ teaspoon salt
1 tablespoon
   chopped chives

Cream the butter and cheese until well blended. Mix in the flour, salt and chives with a fork. Shape the dough into a ball and wrap in plastic wrap. Refrigerate at least 1 hour.

Roll out the dough to ¼-inch thickness on a lightly floured surface. Cut into 1½-inch rounds with a cutter.

Place the crackers 1 inch apart on a greased baking sheet. Bake in a pre-heated 400° oven, 10 minutes (crackers will puff up and shrink slightly). Cool on a wire rack.

Serve plain or with dips and spreads.

About 40 crackers

Devils on Horseback

2 tablespoons butter
1 onion, minced
1 teaspoon dried sage
  leaves
⅓ cup fresh bread
  crumbs
8 oz pitted prunes
10 slices bacon

Melt the butter in a small skillet. Add the onion; cook over low heat until soft. Stir in the sage and bread crumbs. Stuff the prunes with the mixture.

Wrap each prune with ½ strip bacon; secure with wood picks. Cook under a preheated broiler until the bacon is crisp, 4 to 5 minutes on each side.

10 servings

33

Tuna and Parmesan Puffs

½ cup water
3 tablespoons butter
⅓ cup all-purpose
  flour, sifted
2 eggs, beaten
¼ cup grated
  Parmesan cheese
1 can (7 oz) tuna,
  drained
6 tablespoons
  mayonnaise

Heat the water and butter in a medium saucepan over low heat until the butter is melted. Add the flour all at once, beating until the mixture leaves the side of the pan. Let dry over the heat 1 or 2 minutes. Remove from the heat and beat the eggs into the dough, one at a time, beating thoroughly after each addition. Beat in the cheese.

Spoon the dough into a pastry bag fitted with a ½-inch plain tip. Pipe small mounds 2 inches apart on a dampened baking sheet. Bake on the top rack of a 400° oven until crisp and golden, 12 to 15 minutes. Reduce heat to 350° and bake 10 minutes.

Make a small slit in the side of each puff and return to turned-off oven with door ajar for 30 minutes. Mash the tuna with the mayonnaise; spoon into puffs. Serve warm.
25 to 30 puffs

Baby Pizzas

1 package (18 oz) hot
  roll mix
2 tablespoons oil
2 onions, minced
2 cloves garlic,
  minced
1 can (28 oz)
  tomatoes
1 can (6 oz) tomato
  paste
Pinch of sugar
1 teaspoon dried
  basil
1 teaspoon dried
  oregano
Salt and pepper

Make hot roll mix following package directions. Let rise.

Heat the oil in a medium skillet. Add the onions and garlic; cook over low heat until soft. Chop the tomatoes coarsely and add to the skillet with their juice. Add the tomato paste, sugar and herbs. Simmer, stirring occasionally, until the sauce begins to thicken. Add salt and pepper to taste.

Roll out the dough to ¼-inch thickness on a lightly floured surface. Cut into 2½-inch rounds. Arrange on a greased baking sheet. Spoon the tomato sauce onto the dough. Bake in a preheated 425° oven until the dough is puffed and golden, 10 to 15 minutes.

If desired, top with ripe olives, anchovy fillets and chopped parsley.
About 40 pizzas

Cheese and Apricot Whirls

½ package (8-oz size)
    cream cheese,
    softened
3 tablespoons milk
½ cup grated sharp
    Cheddar cheese
Salt and pepper
1 can (16 oz) apricot
    halves, well
    drained

Beat the cream cheese with the milk in a small mixer bowl until fluffy; beat in the Cheddar cheese and salt and pepper to taste.

Spoon the cheese mixture into a pastry bag fitted with a ½-inch star tip. Pipe the cheese into the apricot halves. If desired, sprinkle with paprika and garnish with chopped walnuts.

About 14 servings

Crispy Sausage Balls

12 oz bulk pork
    sausage
1 cup grated sharp
    Cheddar cheese
½ cup rolled oats
¼ teaspoon oregano
¼ teaspoon basil
1 clove garlic,
    minced
Salt and pepper
1 egg, beaten

Mix all ingredients. Shape into 16 meatballs on a floured surface.

Place the meatballs on a baking sheet. Bake in a preheated 375° oven for 30 minutes.

Serve the meatballs hot or cold, with Barbecue Dip (see page 24) or tomato sauce.

16 meatballs

Mini Ham Crepes

¾ cup all-purpose
    flour
Pinch of salt
1 egg
1 cup milk
Vegetable oil
8 oz sliced Swiss
    cheese
3 oz sliced ham
Grated Parmesan
    cheese

Sift the flour and salt into a small bowl. Beat in the egg and milk to make a smooth batter.

Heat enough oil to coat the bottom of a small skillet. Pour in 1 tablespoon batter. Cook over medium heat until bottom is brown; turn and cook other side. Repeat, adding more oil as necessary. Stack crepes separated by waxed paper.

Cut the cheese and ham into small strips. Divide strips among the crepes. Roll up the crepes and arrange in a baking dish. Sprinkle with the Parmesan and heat under the broiler.

About 24 crepes

Cheese Cornets

1 package (17¼ oz)
   frozen puff pastry,
   thawed
1 egg, beaten
½ cup heavy cream,
   whipped
1 cup grated Cheddar
   cheese
½ cup crumbled
   blue cheese
Pinch of cayenne
   pepper
Pinch of dry mustard
1 tablespoon
   chopped parsley
Salt and pepper

Roll out the pastry to a 12-inch square; trim edges. Divide into 12 strips. Dampen one long edge of each strip. Wind strips around 12 greased cornet molds, starting at pointed end and overlapping ¼ inch as you wind. Gently press edges together.

Place the pastry on a dampened baking sheet; brush with beaten egg. Bake in a preheated 450° oven until puffed and golden, 10 to 15 minutes. Remove the molds and return pastry to oven for 5 minutes. Cool on a wire rack.

Mix cream, cheeses, cayenne, mustard, parsley and salt and pepper to taste. Spoon or pipe the mixture into pastry cornets. Garnish with parsley sprigs if desired.

12 cornets

NOTE: If cornet molds are unavailable, cut pastry into 2-inch rounds, brush with egg and bake as directed on package. Sandwich filling between rounds.

Salmon Hazelnut Eclairs

⅓ cup water
4 tablespoons butter
½ cup all-purpose
   flour, sifted
2 eggs, beaten
¼ cup grated
   Cheddar cheese
1 can (7 oz) salmon,
   drained
1 tablespoon capers,
   rinsed
1 teaspoon dry
   sherry
2 tablespoons
   chopped toasted
   hazelnuts
1 tablespoon oil
¾ cup mayonnaise
1 teaspoon lemon
   juice
1 teaspoon dried
   tarragon
½ teaspoon celery
   seeds
¼ teaspoon cumin

Make pastry with the water, butter, flour, salt, pepper, eggs and cheese as directed for Tuna and Parmesan Puffs (see page 35). Spoon the pastry into a pastry bag fitted with a ½-inch plain tip; pipe 2-inch lengths 2 inches apart onto a greased baking sheet.

Bake in a preheated 400° oven until well risen and golden brown, about 20 minutes. Cut a slit in the side of each éclair to allow steam to escape. Cool on wire racks.

Mash the salmon with the capers. Stir in the sherry and hazelnuts until blended. Whisk the oil into the mayonnaise, then stir in the remaining ingredients and add to the salmon. Refrigerate until serving time.

To serve, spoon the salmon filling into the éclairs.

About 18 éclairs

NOTE: Any leftover filling can be served as a dip with vegetable dippers.

Cocktail Kabobs

½ lb pork sausage
  links or
  frankfurters
1 can (8 oz) sliced
  pineapple, drained
½ small cucumber
4 small tomatoes
8 oz Cheddar cheese
12 pitted dates,
  halved

Pan-fry or broil the sausage, turning frequently, until cooked and evenly browned. Cool. Cut into small pieces.

Cut the pineapple and cucumber into ½-inch pieces and the tomatoes into thin wedges. Cube the cheese. Thread pieces of the sausage, pineapple, cucumber, tomato, cheese and dates on wooden skewers or picks.
About 24 Kabobs

Peanut Cheese Cubes

1 package (8 oz)
  cream cheese
2 tablespoons apple
  or orange juice
1 cup grated Cheddar
  cheese
4 oz cooked ham,
  minced
3 green onions,
  finely chopped
1 teaspoon dry
  mustard
1 teaspoon chili
  powder
Dash of hot pepper
  sauce
¾ cup chopped
  peanuts

Beat the cream cheese with juice until fluffy. Beat in the Cheddar cheese, ham, onions, mustard, chili powder and hot pepper sauce.

Shape the mixture into a rectangular block. Wrap in plastic wrap; refrigerate until firm.

Cut the cheese into 1-inch cubes. Toss in peanuts to coat. Arrange on a serving plate and refrigerate until serving time.
About 20 cubes

Sausage Roll-Ups

1 package (2¾ to
  3½ oz) Boursin or
  other semi-soft
  cheese with garlic
½ cup cottage
  cheese
Salt and pepper
½ lb sliced
  mortadella or
  salami

Mix the cheeses to blend, adding salt and pepper to taste. Spread the mixture over the meat slices. Roll up and secure with wood picks. Serve the rolls on a bed of shredded lettuce if desired.
About 20 roll-ups

FRUIT & VEGETABLE STARTERS

Pears in Tarragon Dressing

½ cup mayonnaise
¼ cup half-and-half
2 teaspoons tarragon
   wine vinegar
Salt
Cayenne pepper
2 tablespoons
   chopped fresh
   tarragon
4 pears

Mix the mayonnaise, half-and-half and vinegar in a small bowl. Add salt and cayenne to taste. Stir in the tarragon, mixing well. Cover and refrigerate to blend flavors.

At serving time, peel, halve and core the pears. Place cut side down on individual lettuce-lined plates and spoon the tarragon dressing over each.

4 servings

Melon with Grapes

2 small melons
½ lb green seedless
   grapes, halved
½ cup white wine
½-inch piece
   gingerroot, peeled
   and minced
Superfine sugar

Cut the melons in half, discarding the seeds. Scoop out the flesh with a melon baller or remove in chunks and cut into cubes. Place in a bowl. Reserve melon shells.

Stir the grapes, wine and ginger into the melon balls. Add sugar to taste. Cover and refrigerate 2 hours.

Spoon melon into melon shells. Serve immediately.

4 servings

Melon and Mint Sorbet

¾ cup sugar
5 tablespoons water
Small bunch fresh
    mint or 2
    tablespoons dried
    mint leaves
1 large ripe
    cantaloupe or
    honeydew melon
Grated rind and juice
    of 2 limes or
    lemons
2 egg whites

Heat the sugar and water in a small saucepan, stirring constantly, until the sugar is dissolved. Heat to boiling; reduce heat and simmer 10 minutes. Stir in the mint and let cool.

Cut the melon into chunks and puree in a blender. Strain the mint syrup into the puree and add the lime rind and juice. Pour into a freezer container, cover and freeze until partially frozen, 2 to 3 hours. Transfer to a bowl and beat until smooth. Beat egg whites until stiff; fold into the melon mixture. Return to covered container and freeze until firm.

Transfer to refrigerator 30 minutes before serving to soften slightly. Garnish with mint sprigs if desired

6 servings

Apple and Ginger Sorbet

4 apples, peeled and
    sliced
Grated rind and juice
    of ½ lemon
3 tablespoons brown
    sugar
1 teaspoon ground
    ginger
½-inch piece
    gingerroot,
    peeled and
    minced
4 tablespoons apple
    jelly, melted
⅔ cup ginger ale or
    apple juice
2 egg whites

Cook the apples, lemon rind and juice, covered, over low heat until the apples are very soft. Put through a food mill and add the sugar, ginger and gingerroot; let cool.

Stir in the jelly and ginger ale. Pour into a freezer container; cover and freeze until partially frozen, about 1 hour. Transfer to a bowl and beat until smooth. Beat the egg whites until stiff; fold into the apple mixture. Return to covered container; freeze until firm.

Transfer to refrigerator 30 minutes before serving to soften slightly. Garnish with candied ginger if desired.

6 servings

Tomato and Basil Sorbet

1 can (46 oz) tomato
 juice
Juice of ½ lemon
1 tablespoon
 Worcestershire
 sauce
2 teaspoons finely
 chopped basil or 1
 teaspoon dried
 basil leaves
2 tablespoons dry
 white wine
2 drops hot pepper
 sauce
Salt and pepper
2 egg whites

Mix the tomato juice, lemon juice, Worcestershire and basil, wine and hot pepper sauce; add salt and pepper to taste.

Pour into a freezer container; cover and freeze until partially frozen, about 1½ hours. Transfer the mixture to a bowl and beat until smooth. Return to covered container; freeze for 1 hour and beat again until smooth. Beat egg whites until stiff; fold into tomato mixture. Freeze until firm.

Transfer to refrigerator 30 minutes before serving to soften slightly. Garnish with basil if desired.

6 to 8 servings

Waldorf Salad

1 lb red apples, sliced
Juice of 1 lemon
6 stalks celery, sliced
½ cup mayonnaise
1 teaspoon sugar
¾ cup walnuts,
   coarsely chopped
Lettuce leaves

Toss the apple slices with lemon juice in a large bowl. Add the celery, mayonnaise, sugar and walnuts; mix to combine thoroughly.

Arrange the salad in individual lettuce-lined bowls and refrigerate until ready to serve.
4 to 6 servings

Citrus Endive Salad

4 heads Belgian
   endive
3 oranges
1 grapefruit
4 tablespoons olive
   oil
2 tablespoons lemon
   juice
1 teaspoon Dijon
   mustard
Salt and pepper
2 teaspoons chopped
   parsley
Lettuce leaves

Slice endive into ¼-inch pieces; place in a medium bowl. Peel the oranges and grapefruit and cut into segments, discarding all pith. Add to the endive.

Mix the oil, lemon juice and mustard; add salt and pepper to taste. Stir in the parsley. Pour the dressing over the salad and toss well. Arrange the salad in individual lettuce-lined bowls.
4 servings

Summer Melon Salad

1 lb tomatoes
1 ripe honeydew
   melon, peeled
1 cucumber
4 tablespoons olive
   oil
2 tablespoons lemon
   juice
1 tablespoon each
   chopped parsley,
   tarragon and
   chives
Salt and pepper
Lettuce leaves

Cut half of one tomato into wedges for ganish. Peel and chop the remaining tomatoes, discarding the seeds. Dice the melon and cucumber.

Mix the oil, lemon juice and herbs; add salt and pepper to taste. Toss with the chopped tomatoes, melon and cucumber in a bowl. Cover and refrigerate 2 to 3 hours. Arrange the salad in individual lettuce-lined bowls. Garnish with tomato wedges.
6 servings

Stuffed Pears

½ package (8 oz size) cream cheese
1 tablespoon chopped chives
2 teaspoons chopped parsley
¼ cup finely chopped walnuts
1 apple, grated
2 teaspoons lemon juice
2 small heads Belgian endive
4 pears
4 slices prosciutto

Beat the cream cheese in a small bowl with the herbs and nuts. Stir in the apple and lemon juice.

Arrange the endive leaves on 4 individual plates. Peel, halve and core the pears. Spoon the cheese mixture into the center of each half; arrange two halves on each plate. Garnish with a rolled ham slice. Serve immediately.

4 servings

Prosciutto with Melon

12 very thin slices prosciutto or Black Forest ham
1 small honeydew melon, cut into 4 wedges
8 ripe figs (optional)

Divide the ham among 4 individual plates. Cut melon from the shell in one piece but leave in place. Cut melon crosswise into slices. Place on the ham.

Cut the figs into sections from the stem end almost through to the base; use as garnish if desired.

4 servings

Guacamole

2 ripe avocados
1 clove garlic
½ onion, chopped
1 tablespoon lime juice
4 small tomatoes, peeled, seeded and chopped
2 tablespoons chopped parsley
1 teaspoon chili powder
Hot pepper sauce
Salt

Peel and pit the avocados; cut into chunks. Crush the garlic. Place the avocados, garlic, onion, lime juice, tomatoes and parsley in a blender and puree. Add the chili powder and hot pepper sauce and salt to taste. Refrigerate 1 hour. Serve as a dip with Melba toast or spoon onto lettuce leaves and serve as a salad.

4 to 6 servings

NOTE: Do not prepare more than 1 hour before serving or the gaucamole may discolor.

Rice and Tomato Salad

3 tablespoons
  long-grain rice
4 tomatoes
2 oz mushrooms,
  thinly sliced
10 pitted ripe olives,
  halved
1 tablespoon
  chopped parsley
2 tablespoons oil
1 tablespoon lemon
  juice
½ clove garlic,
  minced
1 teaspoon Dijon
  mustard
2 teaspoons chopped
  basil leaves
1 teaspoon sugar
Salt and pepper

Cook the rice in boiling salted water until tender, 12 to 14 minutes; drain. Cool under cold water and drain well. Peel, seed and chop the tomatoes.

Combine the rice, tomatoes, mushrooms and olives in a bowl; sprinkle with the parsley.

Mix the oil, lemon juice and garlic; whisk in the mustard, basil, sugar and salt and pepper to taste. Spoon the dressing over the salad and toss well.

Transfer to a serving dish. Cover and refrigerate until serving time.

4 servings

Artichokes Vinaigrette

1 can (14 oz)
  artichoke hearts
2 hard-cooked eggs
4 tablespoons olive
  oil
1 tablespoon lemon
  juice
1 teaspoon grated
  lemon rind
1 tablespoon white
  wine
1 teaspoon honey
1 tablespoon
  chopped parsley
1½ teaspoons each
  dried oregano,
  thyme and basil
1 tablespoon capers,
  rinsed

Rinse the artichokes under cold water; drain well. Cut the artichokes and eggs into quarters; arrange on a serving plate.

Whisk the oil with the lemon juice and rind, wine and honey; stir in the herbs.

Spoon the dressing over the salad. Sprinkle with capers. Cover and refrigerate until serving time.

4 to 6 servings

Roasted Pepper Salad

2 each red, green and
    yellow sweet
    peppers
4 tablespoons olive
    oil
2 tablespoons wine
    vinegar
1 teaspoon sugar
1 teaspoon Meaux or
    other coarse-grain
    mustard
Salt and pepper
1 can (2 oz) anchovy
    fillets, drained
Pitted ripe olives

Preheat broiler and broil the peppers as
close to the heat as possible, until the
skin is charred on all sides. Rub off the
skins under cold running water.

Halve and seed the peppers. Slice
into thin strips and arrange on a serving dish.

Whisk the oil with the vinegar,
sugar and mustard. Add salt and pepper to taste. Spoon the dressing over
the peppers. Arrange the anchovies in a
lattice pattern over the salad and garnish with olives. Cover and refrigerate
until serving time.

4 to 6 servings

Shrimp-Stuffed Zucchini

8 small zucchini
1 tablespoon oil
1 clove garlic, minced
2 shallots or green onions, finely chopped
4 tomatoes, chopped
2 drops hot pepper sauce
1 teaspoon dried thyme leaves, crumbled
Salt and pepper
2 jars (4½ oz each) shrimp
2 tablespoons butter
2 tablespoons flour
1 cup milk
1 teaspoon prepared mustard
1 cup grated Cheddar cheese
1 tablespoon grated Parmesan cheese

Blanch the zucchini in boiling salted water 2 minutes; cool under cold water. Halve the zucchini lengthwise and scoop out and chop the pulp. Arrange the shells in a shallow baking dish.

Heat the oil in a medium skillet. Add the garlic and shallots; cook over low heat 5 minutes. Add the tomatoes, zucchini pulp, hot pepper sauce, thyme and salt and pepper. Heat to boiling, then simmer, uncovered, 25 minutes. Add the shrimp and spoon into zucchini shells.

Melt the butter in a small saucepan over medium heat; stir in the flour and cook 1 minute. Stir in the milk slowly. Heat to boiling; cook, stirring constantly, 2 minutes. Stir in the mustard, cheeses and salt and pepper to taste. Spoon sauce over zucchini and bake in a preheated 425° oven until golden, 15 to 20 minutes.
8 servings

Avocado with Curried Sauce

½ cup mayonnaise
2 teaspoons curry
  powder
1 clove garlic,
  minced
½ cup heavy cream
2 drops hot pepper
  sauce
Salt
2 hard-cooked eggs,
  chopped
1 tablespoon
  chopped parsley
2 ripe avocados
Juice of ½ lemon

Mix the mayonnaise with the curry powder and garlic in a small bowl; stir in the cream. Add the hot pepper sauce and the salt to taste. Cover and refrigerate 4 to 6 hours to blend flavors.

Stir the chopped eggs and parsley into the sauce.

Peel the avocados, if liked; cut in half and remove the pits. Sprinkle with lemon juice.

Arrange the avocado halves on 4 individual plates. Spoon the sauce into the halves. Garnish with lemon twists and basil leaves if desired.

4 servings

Marinated Mushrooms

4 tablespoons oil
2 cloves garlic,
  minced
1 small onion, finely
  chopped
2 bay leaves
1 teaspoon each
  dried thyme and
  rosemary
1 tablespoon
  chopped parsley
⅔ cup dry white
  wine
6 peppercorns
12 coriander seeds
Salt
1½ lb button
  mushrooms

Heat the oil in a small saucepan. Add the garlic and onion; cook over low heat, without browning, 10 minutes. Stir in the bay leaves, thyme, rosemary, parsley and wine. Heat to boiling; reduce heat and simmer 2 minutes. Add peppercorns, coriander and salt to taste. Pour the dressing over the mushrooms in a large bowl, tossing well to coat. Cover and refrigerate 3 to 4 hours, stirring occasionally.

Spoon the marinated mushrooms into a serving dish. Sprinkle with chopped parsley if desired, and serve with French bread.

6 servings

Crispy Mushrooms with Herb and Garlic Mayonnaise

¾ cup all-purpose
   flour
Pinch of salt
1 tablespoon oil
½ cup water
2 egg whites
1 lb button
   mushrooms
Vegetable oil
½ cup mayonnaise
1 to 2 cloves garlic,
   minced
2 tablespoons
   chopped parsley
1 tablespoon
   chopped fresh
   basil or 1½
   teaspoons dried

Combine the flour and salt in a large bowl; slowly beat in 1 tablespoon oil and the water. Beat egg whites until stiff; fold into the batter.

Drop the mushrooms into the batter, tossing to coat. Heat oil in a deep fryer to 375°. Fry the mushrooms in batches, using a slotted spoon to lift them from the batter into the oil. Drain on paper towels and keep hot while frying the remainder.

Mix the mayonnaise, garlic and herbs; spoon into a serving bowl. Serve with the hot mushrooms.

4 to 6 servings

Lima Beans à la Grecque

2 tablespoons oil
1 clove garlic, thinly sliced
1 onion, minced
8 tomatoes, peeled, seeded and chopped
2 tablespoons dry white wine
1 tablespoon chopped parsley
1 bay leaf
Salt and pepper
2 packages (10 oz each) frozen lima beans

Heat the oil in a large saucepan. Add the garlic and onion; cook over low heat 5 minutes. Add the remaining ingredients except the beans. Cover and simmer 10 minutes. Add the beans and cook until tender. Remove the bay leaf. Let stand to cool; refrigerate until serving time.

4 servings

Eggplant Cheesecake

1 eggplant (12 oz), diced
Salt
4 tablespoons butter
1 cup crushed cheese crackers
1 tablespoon grated Parmesan cheese
4 tablespoons oil
1 onion, thinly sliced
1 package (8 oz) cream cheese, softened
⅔ cup sour cream
Salt and pepper
¼ teaspoon each dried thyme, oregano and basil
3 eggs, beaten
1½ cups grated Cheddar cheese

Place the eggplant in a large colander, sprinkle generously with salt and let stand 1 hour.

Melt the butter in a small saucepan. Stir in the crackers and Parmesan cheese and press the mixture into the bottom of a greased 8-inch springform pan.

Heat the oil in a medium skillet. Add the onion and cook until lightly browned. Remove with a slotted spoon and reserve.

Rinse the eggplant under cold water and pat dry. Add to the skillet and cook until lightly browned. Drain on paper towels.

Mix the cream cheese and sour cream in a large bowl, adding salt and pepper to taste. Stir in the herbs, eggs and Cheddar cheese. Add the onion and eggplant; combine thoroughly.

Spread the eggplant mixture in the springform pan. Bake in a preheated 375° oven until set and golden brown, 35 to 40 minutes. Serve hot or cold.

12 servings

Leek Soufflé

4 tablespoons butter
1 lb leeks, cleaned
    and thinly sliced
3 tablespoons flour
½ cup milk
1 cup grated sharp
    Cheddar cheese
1 tablespoon grated
    Parmesan cheese
1 teaspoon prepared
    mustard
Salt and pepper
6 eggs, separated

Melt half the butter in a medium skillet over medium heat. Add the leeks, tossing to coat; cook until soft, 5 to 7 minutes.

Melt the remaining butter in a large saucepan over medium heat; stir in the flour and cook 1 minute. Add the milk slowly, stirring constantly. Cook, stirring constantly, 1 minute. Add the cheeses, mustard and salt and pepper to taste; stir until the cheeses melt; let cool 5 minutes. Beat in the egg yolks. Transfer the leeks with a slotted spoon and stir into the sauce.

Beat the egg whites until stiff; fold into the sauce. Pour into a greased 1-quart soufflé dish. Bake in a preheated 350° oven until risen and golden brown, 35 to 40 minutes. Serve immediately on warmed plates.

4 to 6 servings

Zucchini Strata

1 lb zucchini
Salt
1 lb tomatoes
4 tablespoons oil
1 clove garlic, chopped
1 onion, chopped
1 bay leaf
1 teaspoon dried basil
½ teaspoon dried thyme
3 tablespoons dry white wine
1 teaspoon Worcestershire
1 tablespoon tomato paste
Pinch of sugar
¼ lb mozzarella cheese, sliced
2 tablespoons each grated Parmesan and bread crumbs

Slice the zucchini and place in a colander; sprinkle with salt and let stand 1 hour. Peel, seed and finely chop the tomatoes.

Heat 1 tablespoon of the oil in a medium saucepan. Add the garlic and onion and cook until soft. Add the tomatoes and cook 2 minutes. Add the herbs, wine, Worcestershire, tomato paste and sugar; simmer, uncovered, until thickened, about 45 minutes. Remove bay leaf.

Rinse the zucchini under cold water and pat dry. Heat the remaining oil in a skillet. Add the zucchini and sauté until golden. Drain.

Layer the zucchini, mozzarella and tomato sauce in a 9-inch square baking dish. Sprinkle with grated Parmesan and bread crumbs. Bake in a preheated 400° oven 30 minutes. Serve hot or cold.

6 to 8 servings

Tartlets Niçoise

2 cups all-purpose
flour
Pinch of salt
4 tablespoons
shortening
6 tablespoons butter
1/4 cup grated
Parmesan cheese
1 to 2 tablespoons
ice water
2 onions, sliced
3 medium tomatoes,
thickly sliced
12 anchovy fillets
24 pitted ripe olives
1 to 2 tablespoons
olive oil

Combine the flour and salt in a bowl and cut in the shortening and 4 tablespoons of the butter until the mixture resembles fine crumbs. Stir in the cheese. Mix in enough water to make a firm dough. Cover and refrigerate 15 minutes. Knead lightly. Roll out to 1/8-inch thickness on a lightly floured surface. Cut circles to line six 3-inch tart pans. Ease the pastry into the pans; prick with a fork. Refrigerate about 30 minutes.

Melt the remaining butter in a skillet and lightly brown the onions; let cool.

Divide the onions among the pastry pans; cover with the tomatoes and decorate with the anchovies and sliced ripe olives. Sprinkle lightly with the olive oil.

Bake in a preheated 350° oven until the pastry is golden, 25 to 30 minutes. Serve hot or cold.

6 servings

Ratatouille Tartlets

1½ cups all-purpose
flour
Pinch of salt
4 tablespoons
shortening
4 tablespoons butter
1 to 2 tablespoons
ice water

FILLING:

1 tablespoon butter
1 clove garlic, thinly
sliced
1 onion, sliced
1 small eggplant,
chopped
1 zucchini, sliced
4 tomatoes, seeded
and chopped
1 tablespoon tomato
paste
Salt and pepper

Make pastry and refrigerate as for Tartlets Niçoise (opposite), omitting the cheese. Knead lightly. Roll out on a lightly floured surface to ⅛-inch thickness. Cut circles to fit six 3-inch tart pans. Ease the pastry into the pans and prick with a fork. Refrigerate about 30 minutes.

Melt 1 tablespoon butter in a large saucepan. Add the garlic and onion; cook 5 to 10 minutes. Stir in remaining ingredients; simmer, covered, until eggplant is soft, 20 to 30 minutes.

Line pastry shells with aluminum foil and fill with dried beans. Bake in a preheated 400° oven until golden brown, about 12 minutes. Remove the foil and beans; return pastries to oven for 5 minutes.

Spoon the warm ratatouille into the pastry shells and serve immediately, or cool the ratatouille and spoon into the shells just before serving.

6 servings

Quiche Provençale

2 cups all-purpose
  flour
Pinch of salt
8 tablespoons butter
2 tablespoons
  shortening
1 egg yolk
Ice water
1 onion, sliced
1 clove garlic,
  minced
2 oz mushrooms,
  sliced
1 zucchini, diced
2 tomatoes, peeled
  and chopped
1 teaspoon dried
  basil
½ teaspoon each
  dried oregano and
  rosemary
Salt and pepper
2 eggs
⅔ cup half-and-half
½ cup grated
  Cheddar cheese
1 oz Swiss cheese,
  sliced

Combine the flour and salt in a bowl
and cut in 6 tablespoons of the butter
and the shortening until the mixture
resembles fine crumbs. Stir in the egg
yolk and enough water to make a firm
dough. Knead lightly.

Roll out the pastry to a 10-inch circle
on a lightly floured surface. Ease the
pastry into a 9-inch quiche pan, pressing evenly around side; trim edge.
Prick all over; refrigerate 30 minutes.
Line pastry with foil; fill with dried
beans. Bake in a preheated 375° oven
12 to 15 minutes. Remove foil and
beans; return the pastry to the oven
for 5 minutes.

Melt the remaining butter in a skillet and cook the onion and garlic over
low heat 5 minutes. Add the vegetables, herbs and salt and pepper to
taste; cook 10 minutes.

Beat the eggs and cream; stir in the
Cheddar cheese. Spoon the vegetable
mixture into the pastry shell; pour in
the egg mixture. Arrange sliced cheese
on top. Bake at 375° until set, 25 to 30
minutes. Serve hot or cold.

6 to 8 servings

Quiche Paysanne

¾ cup all-purpose
  flour
½ cup whole wheat
  flour
Pinch of salt
6 tablespoons butter
4 to 5 tablespoons
  ice water
5 slices bacon
1 large onion,
  chopped
2 potatoes, sliced
2 eggs
⅔ cup heavy cream
1 tablespoon each
  chopped parsley
  and chives
½ teaspoon salt
¼ teaspoon ground
  pepper
½ red sweet pepper,
  seeded and
  chopped
¾ cup grated
  Cheddar cheese

Combine the flours and salt in a bowl
and cut in the butter until the mixture
resembles fine crumbs. Add enough
water to make a firm dough. Knead
lightly.

Roll out pastry to a 10-inch circle on
a lightly floured surface. Ease the pastry into a 9-inch quiche pan, pressing
evenly around the side; trim edge.
Prick all over; refrigerate 30 minutes.
Line pastry with foil and fill with dried
beans. Bake in a preheated 375° oven
until set, 12 to 15 minutes. Remove
the foil and beans and return the pastry
to the oven for 5 minutes.

Cook the bacon until crisp; remove
and crumble. Add the onion and potatoes to the bacon drippings and cook
until browned, 12 to 15 minutes.
Drain.

Beat eggs and cream. Stir in the
herbs, salt and pepper. Spoon the potatoes and onion into the pastry shell;
sprinkle with bacon and red pepper.
Pour in the egg mixture and sprinkle
with cheese. Bake in a 375° oven for
20 to 25 minutes. Serve hot or cold.

6 to 8 servings

Tomato Cheese Tarts

1 cup all-purpose
  flour
Pinch of salt
¾ cup grated sharp
  Cheddar cheese
1 tablespoon grated
  Parmesan cheese
3 egg yolks
½ cup butter,
  softened, cut into
  pieces
3 medium tomatoes,
  peeled and sliced
2 tablespoons
  chopped parsley
1 tablespoon each
  dried basil and
  thyme
2 oz Swiss cheese,
  sliced

Combine the flour and salt in a bowl and make a well in the center; place the grated cheeses, egg yolks and butter in the well and gradually work into the flour. Knead lightly. Shape into a ball, cover and refrigerate 1 hour.

Roll out dough to ⅛-inch thickness on a lightly floured surface. Cut 8 circles to fit 3-inch tart pans. Line pans with dough; refrigerate 20 minutes. Line pastry with foil; fill with dried beans and bake in a preheated 400° oven 20 minutes. Remove foil and beans and return pastry to oven for 5 minutes.

Layer tomato slices in pastry, sprinkling each layer with herbs. Top with the Swiss cheese. Bake in a 400° oven until cheese is bubbly, about 5 minutes. Let cool before serving.
8 servings

Brittany Crepes

2 eggs
1 cup milk
1 cup water
¾ cup all-purpose flour
¾ cup whole wheat flour
Pinch of salt
Vegetable oil
2 cloves garlic, thinly sliced
1 large onion, sliced
1 green pepper, seeded and thinly sliced
1 medium eggplant, chopped
4 tomatoes, peeled and chopped
1 teaspoon each dried basil and oregano
1 tablespoon chopped parsley
Salt and pepper
2 tablespoons grated Parmesan cheese

Combine the eggs, milk, water, flours and salt in a blender and whirl until smooth. Let stand 30 minutes.

Heat a lightly oiled 6-inch crepe pan or skillet over medium heat. Pour in just enough batter to cover the bottom, pouring any excess back. Cook the crepe until brown, 2 to 3 minutes; turn and cook the other side until golden. Repeat with remaining batter, stacking crepes between waxed paper and keeping warm.

Heat 1 tablespoon oil in a skillet and cook the garlic and onion over low heat 5 minutes. Add the remaining ingredients except cheese; cook until the eggplant is soft, about 15 minutes.

Divide the vegetable mixture among the crepes; sprinkle with the cheese and roll up crepes, tucking ends under. Place on a greased baking sheet and bake in a preheated 400° oven until crisp, 30 to 35 minutes. Serve hot.

About 20 crepes

FISH & SHELLFISH STARTERS

Trout with Ham and Garlic

4 slices prosciutto or Black Forest ham
4 trout, cleaned
Salt and pepper
4 tablespoons olive oil
2 cloves garlic, thinly sliced
Grated rind and juice of 1 lemon
2 tablespoons chopped parsley
Lemon wedges

Roll up ham slices; place 1 slice in the cavity of each trout. Season fish with salt and pepper.

Heat the oil in a large skillet over medium heat. Add the garlic and trout and sauté the trout 5 to 8 minutes on each side, or until they flake when tested with a fork. Drain on paper towels and keep warm. Add lemon rind and juice to skillet; cook 1 minute.

Arrange the trout on warm plates and spoon the sauce over them. Sprinkle with the chopped parsley and serve with lemon wedges.

4 servings

Mussels Antipasto

4 lb mussels, scrubbed

3 cloves garlic, minced

2 teaspoons grated lemon rind

3 tablespoons chopped parsley

1 teaspoon dried basil

½ teaspoon dried thyme

¼ cup fresh white bread crumbs

5 tablespoons oil

Steam the mussels, covered, in 1 cup boiling water until the shells open, 5 to 10 minutes; discard any mussels that do not open. Drain.

Discard the empty half shell from each mussel. Arrange the mussels on half shells in a large shallow baking dish or individual ovenproof dishes.

Mix the garlic, lemon rind, chopped parsley, basil, thyme and bread crumbs; sprinkle over the mussels. Spoon oil over. Place under a preheated broiler until pale golden, 5 to 7 minutes; do not overcook or the mussels will toughen.

4 to 6 servings

Mussels in Curry Sauce

4 lb mussels,
    scrubbed
2 tablespoons butter
1 small onion, finely
    chopped
1 teaspoon curry
    powder
1 teaspoon tomato
    paste
4 tablespoons dry
    white wine
2 tablespoons
    apricot jam,
    strained
½ cup heavy cream
½ cup mayonnaise
Juice of ½ lemon
Salt and pepper
4 cups cold cooked
    rice

Steam the mussels, covered, in 1 cup boiling water until the shells open, about 5 to 10 minutes; discard any mussels that do not open. Drain. Reserve 4 to 6 whole mussels for garnish; remove the remainder from their shells, being careful not to crush them.

Melt the butter in a small saucepan over low heat. Add the onion and cook 3 minutes.

Stir in the curry powder; cook for 3 minutes. Stir in the tomato paste, wine and jam. Let stand to cool.

Whip cream to soft peaks and fold into the sauce. Stir in the mayonnaise and lemon juice and season to taste with salt and pepper. Cover and refrigerate 2 to 3 hours.

Just before serving, fold the shelled mussels into the sauce. Serve over rice on chilled plates. Garnish with the reserved mussels.

4 to 6 servings

Seafood Salad

6 sea scallops,
   quartered
12 oz shrimp, peeled
   and deveined
12 mussels,
   scrubbed
1 can (6 oz)
   crabmeat, drained
4 tablespoons olive
   oil
2 tablespoons lemon
   juice
1 clove garlic,
   minced
2 tablespoons
   chopped parsley
Salt and pepper
Lemon slices

Cook scallops in 1 cup boiling water just until they turn opaque, 2 to 3 minutes. Remove with slotted spoon. Add shrimp; cook just until they turn pink, 4 to 5 minutes. Remove with slotted spoon. Add mussels; cook until shells open, 5 to 10 minutes. Discard any mussels that do not open. Drain mussels and remove top shells. Place the cooked seafood and the crabmeat in a serving dish.

Whisk the oil, lemon juice, garlic and parsley with salt and pepper to taste in a small bowl. Pour over the seafood and toss. Cover and refrigerate 30 minutes. Serve with lemon slices.

4 to 6 servings

Fritto Misto di Mare

¾ cup all-purpose
  flour
Pinch of salt
2 tablespoons olive
  oil
½ cup water
1 large egg white,
  beaten until stiff
Vegetable oil
6 sea scallops, cut in
  half
6 large shrimp,
  shelled and
  deveined
⅔ lb sole fillets, cut
  into 2-inch strips
Lemon slices or
  wedges

Sift the flour and salt into a bowl; stir in the olive oil and water slowly. Fold in the egg white.

Heat the vegetable oil in a deep fryer to 375°. Dip small batches of each type of seafood into batter; lift into the oil with a slotted spoon. Fry until golden brown. Drain on paper towels; keep the cooked food hot while frying the remaining seafood.

Arrange the fritto misto on a warmed serving dish with lemon slices or wedges.

6 servings

Grilled Crab

2 cans (6 oz each) crabmeat, drained
Juice of ½ lemon
2 tablespoons butter
1 small onion, finely chopped
½ cup dry sherry
1 teaspoon Worcestershire sauce
1 teaspoon Dijon mustard
1 teaspoon dried thyme leaves
2 teaspoons chopped parsley
1¼ cups heavy cream
2 tablespoons fresh bread crumbs
1 tablespoon grated Parmesan cheese

Flake the crabmeat into a bowl; add the lemon juice.

Melt the butter in a medium saucepan. Add the onion and sauté until golden. Pour in the sherry and boil to reduce to 2 tablespoons. Reduce heat and stir in the Worcestershire, mustard and herbs. Add the cream and cook until thickened. Stir in the crab. Season to taste with salt and pepper.

Spoon the mixture into small ovenproof ramekins and sprinkle with bread crumbs and Parmesan cheese. Place under a preheated broiler until bubbling and golden brown. Serve hot, garnished with lemon halves if desired.

4 servings

71

Cheese and Shrimp Soufflés

2 cans (2 oz each) anchovy fillets
1 tablespoon oil
2 cloves garlic, minced
1 tablespoon minced parsley
2 large eggs, separated
⅔ cup half-and-half
1 teaspoon hot mustard
Pinch of cayenne pepper
Salt
3 oz salad shrimp
1 cup grated sharp Cheddar cheese
1 tablespoon grated Parmesan cheese
4 slices French bread, toasted

Drain the anchovies and mash with the oil, garlic and parsley to a smooth paste; reserve.

Beat the egg yolks, half-and-half, mustard, cayenne and salt to taste. Stir in the shrimp and cheeses. Beat egg whites until stiff; fold into egg yolk mixture.

Lightly grease four 4-oz ovenproof ramekins. Divide the shrimp mixture among them. Bake in a preheated 400° oven until risen and golden brown, 12 to 15 minutes.

Meanwhile, spread the toasted French bread with the reserved anchovy paste. Place under broiler to heat through. Serve immediately with the soufflés.

4 servings

Shrimp Pilaf

4 tablespoons butter
1 small onion, finely
   chopped
1 clove garlic,
   minced
1 cup long-grain rice
⅔ cup dry white
   wine
Pinch of saffron or
   turmeric
2 cups fish stock or
   chicken broth
Salt and pepper
4 tomatoes, peeled,
   seeded and
   chopped
1½ teaspoons
   chopped fresh
   basil or ½ teaspoon
   dried basil
1 package (8 oz)
   frozen cooked
   shrimp

Melt the butter in a medium skillet. Add the onion and garlic and cook over low heat 5 minutes. Add the rice, stirring to coat with butter. Add the wine and saffron and heat to boiling. Cook, stirring constantly, until most of the wine evaporates.

Stir in 1⅓ cups stock and salt and pepper to taste. Heat to boiling; reduce heat and simmer, covered, for 10 minutes; add more stock if necessary. Stir in the tomatoes, basil and shrimp; cook until the shrimp are heated through and the rice is tender.

Spoon the pilaf into a warmed serving dish. Garnish with basil leaves if desired.

6 servings

Shrimp and Scallops

2 tablespoons butter
2 tablespoons oil
2 cloves garlic,
 chopped
½ lb shrimp, peeled
 and deveined
8 sea scallops, halved
2 tablespoons
 chopped parsley
Juice of ½ lemon

Heat the butter and oil in a medium skillet over medium-high heat. Add the garlic and sauté 2 minutes. Add the shrimp and scallops; sauté until the scallops become opaque and the shrimp turn pink, 2 to 3 minutes.

Stir in the parsley and lemon juice and serve.

4 to 6 servings

Shrimp Roulade

¾ cup all-purpose
 flour
6 eggs, separated
3 tablespoons water
1½ cups grated
 Cheddar cheese
6 tablespoons grated
 Parmesan cheese
Salt and pepper
3 tablespoons butter
1 cup milk
½ lb shrimp, cooked,
 peeled and
 chopped
1 package (2 oz)
 sliced ham,
 chopped
1 hard-cooked egg,
 chopped
2 tablespoons
 chopped parsley

Sift ½ cup of the flour into a large bowl; beat in the egg yolks and water until smooth. Stir in the Cheddar cheese, half of the Parmesan cheese and salt and pepper. Beat the egg whites until stiff; fold into the egg yolk mixture.

Spread the batter evenly in a lined and greased 10 × 15-inch jelly roll pan. Bake in a preheated 400° oven until puffed and golden, 12 to 15 minutes.

Melt the butter in a skillet over medium heat. Stir in the remaining ¼ cup flour; cook 1 minute, stirring constantly. Stir in the milk slowly; cook, stirring, 1 minute. Season with salt and pepper. Stir in the shrimp, ham, chopped egg and parsley.

Invert the roulade onto a sheet of waxed paper sprinkled with the remaining Parmesan. Remove the pan lining paper. Spread the filling evenly over the roulade; roll up like a jelly roll, starting from the short end.

Serve slices hot, garnished with parsley or fresh herbs.

8 servings

Shrimp in Dill Butter

4 tablespoons butter
1 lb shrimp, peeled
  and deveined
Juice of ½ lemon
Chopped dill
Salt and pepper

Melt the butter in a large skillet and sauté the shrimp until they turn pink. Add the lemon juice and season to taste with dill, salt and pepper. Serve with the sauce poured over the shrimp.
4 servings

Herbed Tuna Crepes

¾ cup all-purpose
  flour
Pinch of salt
1 egg
1 cup milk
2 tablespoons cold
  water
Vegetable oil
4 tablespoons butter
1 small onion, finely
  chopped
¼ cup all-purpose
  flour
1 cup milk
6 tablespoons heavy
  cream
1 tablespoons lemon
  juice
1 tablespoon
  chopped chives
1 tablespoon
  chopped parsley
½ teaspoon dried
  rosemary
¼ teaspoon dried
  thyme
1 cup grated Cheddar
  cheese
Pepper
2 cans (6¼ oz each)
  tuna in water,
  drained
Salt
2 tablespoons grated
  Parmesan cheese

Sift the ¾ cup flour and a pinch of salt into a bowl. Make a well in the center and add the egg and ½ cup of the milk; beat into the flour until smooth. Gradually beat in ½ cup milk and 2 tablespoons cold water; beat until smooth.

Heat enough oil to coat the bottom of a 6- or 7-inch crepe pan or skillet over medium-high heat. Pour in about 2 tablespoons batter, tilting the pan to coat the bottom evenly. Cook until browned; turn and brown the other side. Repeat with the remaining batter, stacking the crepes between sheets of waxed paper; keep warm.

Melt the butter in a medium skillet and cook the onion over low heat for 5 minutes. Stir in ¼ cup flour; cook 1 minute. Gradually add 1 cup milk, stirring constantly. Heat to boiling; cook 2 minutes. Reduce heat; stir in the cream, lemon juice, herbs, Cheddar cheese and pepper to taste. Stir until the cheese is melted. Stir in the tuna and add salt to taste.

Divide the filling among the crepes and roll up. Arrange in a lightly greased shallow baking dish and sprinkle with Parmesan cheese. Cover with foil and bake in a preheated 350° oven until hot, about 20 minutes. Remove the foil and return the crepes to the oven until lightly browned, 5 minutes.
12 crepes

Scallop-Shrimp Salad

4 sea scallops
4 tablespoons dry
   white wine
1 sprig parsley
¼ small onion
1 strip lemon rind
1 package (5 oz)
   frozen cooked
   baby shrimp,
   thawed
½ lb mushrooms,
   thinly sliced
6 tablespoons olive
   oil
2 tablespoons lime
   or lemon juice
½ clove garlic,
   minced
1 teaspoon chopped
   parsley
Pepper and salt
Lettuce leaves

Slice the scallops crosswise. Cook the wine, parsley sprig, onion, lemon rind and scallops in a small skillet over medium heat 2 minutes. Remove the scallops to a medium bowl with a slotted spoon; let cool. Stir in the shrimp.

Place the mushrooms in a small bowl and add the oil and lime juice. Sprinkle with garlic, parsley and a liberal amount of pepper. Toss well; let stand 30 minutes. Add salt to taste. Stir the mushrooms into the seafood.

Spoon the salad onto lettuce-lined individual serving dishes. Refrigerate until serving time.

4 servings

Crab Cheese Fries

4 tablespoons butter
6 tablespoons flour
1½ cups milk
Salt and pepper
Grated nutmeg
2 cups grated Swiss
  cheese
4 tablespoons grated
  Parmesan cheese
1 can (6 oz)
  crabmeat, drained
  and flaked
2 egg yolks, beaten
2 eggs
4 tablespoons milk
Fresh bread crumbs
Vegetable oil

Melt the butter in a medium saucepan over medium heat; stir in the flour. Cook, stirring constantly, 2 minutes. Add the 1½ cups milk slowly, stirring constantly. Heat to boiling; add the salt, pepper and nutmeg to taste. Reduce heat; stir in the cheeses until melted. Remove from heat.

Mix in the crabmeat and egg yolks. Spread the mixture ½ inch thick in a lightly oiled 8-inch square baking pan. Cover with aluminum foil; refrigerate until firm, 3 to 4 hours.

Cut the mixture into 1½-inch-long rectangles. Beat the eggs with 4 tablespoons milk. Dip the pieces into the egg, then into crumbs. Heat oil in a deep fryer to 375°. Fry the pieces in small batches until crisp and golden. Serve hot.

About 40 pieces

PÂTÉS, TERRINES & MOUSSES

Smoked Salmon Pâté

4 tablespoons butter, softened
6 tablespoons lemon juice
3 to 4 oz smoked salmon, minced
1 can (3½ oz) salmon, drained
Salt
Cayenne pepper
Dash of hot pepper sauce
1 tablespoon chopped chives
1 tablespoon chopped parsley

Cream the butter with 2 tablespoons of the lemon juice; beat in the smoked and canned salmon. Add salt and cayenne to taste. Mix in hot pepper sauce and remaining lemon juice, beating until the pâté is thick and creamy. Stir in the chives and parsley. Cover and refrigerate until serving time.

Spoon the pâté onto individual serving dishes. Garnish with lemon slices if desired, and serve with toast.

4 servings

Smoked Fish Pâté

8 oz smoked
   mackerel, white-
   fish, trout or other
   smoked fish fillets
2 tablespoons butter
1 small onion, finely
   chopped
2 tablespoons flour
½ cup milk
2 teaspoons lemon
   juice
1 tablespoon dry
   white wine
Salt and pepper
½ cup heavy cream,
   whipped

Remove the skin and any bones from the fish; flake the fish. Melt the butter in a saucepan over low heat. Add the onion and cook until soft, 5 to 7 minutes. Stir in the flour; cook 2 minutes. Stir in the milk slowly; cook, stirring constantly, 1 minute.

Transfer the sauce to a bowl and stir in the lemon juice, wine and salt and pepper to taste. Add the fish and beat until smooth. Fold in the cream. Cover and refrigerate until serving time.

Spoon the pâté onto individual serving plates lined with lettuce leaves. Garnish with cucumber slices.

4 servings

Ardennes Pâté

1 lb boneless pork, diced
8 oz ground veal
12 oz chicken livers, chopped
4 tablespoons brandy
1 teaspoon dried thyme
1 tablespoon green peppercorns (optional)
1 teaspoon salt
½ teaspoon pepper
4 to 6 slices bacon
lemon slices

Mix the pork, veal and chicken livers in a bowl. Stir in the brandy, thyme, green peppercorns, salt and pepper. Cover and refrigerate 2 hours.

Spoon the mixture into a lightly greased 9 ×5 × 3-inch loaf pan. Cover the pâté with bacon slices. Cover the pan with foil; place in roasting pan half-filled with hot water. Bake in a preheated 350° oven 1½ hours.

Cool the pâté in its pan; refrigerate until serving time. Unmold onto a serving plate. Garnish with lemon slices and serve sliced, with toast, French bread or crackers.

8 to 12 servings

Sherried Liver Pâté

4 tablespoons butter
4 oz Canadian bacon, chopped
2 cloves garlic, chopped
1 small onion, chopped
1 lb chicken livers, chopped
2 teaspoons minced parsley
½ teaspoon dried thyme
4 oz mushrooms, chopped
4 tablespoons dry sherry
4 tablespoons heavy cream
1 teaspoon lemon juice
Salt and pepper

Melt butter in a medium skillet over medium heat. Add the bacon, garlic and onion; cook 3 minutes. Stir in the chicken livers; cook 5 minutes. Stir in the herbs and mushrooms. Add the sherry and cook until the liquid evaporates. Cool; puree in a blender. Stir in the cream and lemon juice and season to taste with salt and pepper.

Spoon the pâté into a greased 1-quart baking dish; cover with a lid or foil. Place in a roasting pan half-filled with water. Bake in a preheated 300° oven until the pâté is firm and juices run clear, 2 to 2½ hours. Let stand to cool; refrigerate until serving time.

Scoop the pâté onto individual plates and serve with toast.

6 servings

Pork and Thyme Terrine

6 slices bacon
12 oz ground pork
8 oz pork liver, cut
    into pieces
4 oz pork sausage
    meat
1 medium onion, cut
    into eighths
1 clove garlic
1 teaspoon dried
    thyme
1 tablespoon
    chopped parsley
1 teaspoon salt
½ teaspoon pepper

Line a 9 × 5 × 3-inch loaf pan with the bacon. Place the remaining ingredients in a food processor fitted with a steel blade. Process until mixture is thoroughly combined. Spoon into the loaf pan and cover tightly with aluminum foil.

Place loaf pan in a roasting pan half filled with water. Bake in a preheated 325° oven until juices run clear when loaf is pierced with a fork, 1¼ to 1½ hours.

Remove foil and cover terrine with waxed paper. Weight top with heavy cans. Cool; remove weight. Refrigerate overnight. Unmold and serve sliced, with French bread.

About 18 thin slices

Farmhouse Terrine

1 lb sliced bacon
½ lb pork liver, cut
    into pieces
½ lb ground veal
1 medium onion, cut
    into eighths
4 slices whole wheat
    bread, cut into
    cubes
2 tablespoons
    chopped parsley
1 clove garlic,
    crushed
1 egg
1 teaspoon salt
½ teaspoon pepper
1 bay leaf

Line a 3-cup terrine with one third of the bacon. Chop another third of the bacon. Place the chopped bacon, pork liver, veal, onion, bread, parsley and garlic in a food processor fitted with a steel blade. Process until mixture is thoroughly combined. Add egg, salt and pepper; process to blend.

Spread half of the meat mixture in terrine; cover with bacon slices. Repeat with remaining meat mixture and bacon strips. Place bay leaf on top. Cover tightly with foil.

Place in a roasting pan half-filled with hot water. Bake in a preheated 325° oven until juices run clear when loaf is pierced with a fork, 1¼ to 1½ hours. Remove foil; cover terrine with waxed paper. Weight top with heavy cans. Cool; remove weight. Refrigerate overnight. Serve with French bread.

About 2½ cups

Mediterranean Pâté

3 tablespoons butter
4 green onions, chopped
1 stalk celery, finely chopped
1 can (7 oz) tuna, drained
2 tomatoes, coarsely chopped
2 tablespoons mayonnaise
2 teaspoons lemon juice
Salt and pepper
1 tablespoon green peppercorns or capers, rinsed and drained

Melt the butter in a small skillet over low heat. Add the green onions and celery; cook, without browning, 5 minutes. Let cool.

Place the onion mixture, tuna, tomatoes, mayonnaise and lemon juice in a blender; puree until smooth. Stir in salt and pepper to taste and the peppercorns.

Spoon into a serving dish. Serve with crusty bread or Melba toast.

About 1½ cups

86

Chicken Tarragon Pâté

8 slices bacon
1 lb boned chicken, diced
8 oz ground pork
4 oz pork fat, diced
1 medium onion, finely chopped
1 clove garlic, minced
1 tablespoon green peppercorns
3 tablespoons brandy
3 tablespoons dry vermouth
1 egg, beaten
2 tablespoons chopped fresh tarragon or 1 tablespoon dried
Salt and pepper

Line a 9 × 5 × 3-inch loaf pan with bacon slices. Mix the remaining ingredients until well blended. Place in pan; smooth top.

Place a lightly buttered piece of waxed paper over the pâté and cover tightly with foil. Place the pan in a roasting pan half-filled with hot water. Bake in a preheated 325° oven until the juices run clear when the pâté is pierced with a fork, 2 to 2¼ hours. Let cool 1 hour.

Weight the pâté with heavy cans. Let stand until completely cool. Remove weights; refrigerate until serving time. Unmold to serve.

About 18 thin slices

Duck Terrine

1 duckling (3 lb),
  skinned and boned
1 lb finely ground
  pork
12 oz finely ground
  veal
1 clove garlic,
  minced
1 tablespoon
  Worcestershire
  sauce
Juice of 1 orange
1 teaspoon dried
  marjoram
½ teaspoon each
  dried thyme and
  sage
½ cup dry red wine
Salt and pepper
10 slices bacon
1 tablespoon brandy

Dice the duck and mix with the pork and veal in a large bowl. Stir in the garlic, Worcestershire, orange juice, herbs, wine and salt and pepper to taste. Cover and refrigerate overnight.

Line a $9 \times 5 \times 3$-inch loaf pan with bacon. Press the meat mixture into the terrine, sprinkle with brandy and cover with foil.

Place the loaf pan in a roasting pan filled with 1 inch of hot water. Bake in a preheated 350° oven until the juices run clear when pâté is pierced with a fork, 1½ to 1¾ hours.

Let stand until cool; refrigerate until serving time. Unmold onto a serving plate and serve with French bread. Garnish with orange slices if desired.
8 servings

Chicken Terrine

3 tablespoons butter
2 oz mushrooms, chopped
1 clove garlic, chopped
1 lb chicken livers, chopped
3 tablespoons dry red wine
½ teaspoon dried thyme
Salt
1 tablespoon brandy
1 tablespoon half-and-half
½ lb boneless chicken breast, sliced
2 tablespoons green peppercorns, drained

Melt half of the butter in a medium skillet over medium heat. Add the mushrooms; cook 2 minutes. Remove with a slotted spoon and reserve. Add the remaining butter and the garlic and cook 1 minute. Add the livers; cook 5 minutes. Add the wine, thyme and salt to taste; cook 15 minutes.

Place the chicken liver mixture in a blender and puree. Stir in the reserved mushrooms, the brandy and cream.

Spread a thin layer of the liver mixture in a lightly greased 2-cup oven-proof mold. Cover with half of the chicken and sprinkle with half of the green peppercorns. Repeat the layers of liver, chicken and peppercorns, ending with the liver. Cover with foil.

Place the mold in a roasting pan half-filled with hot water. Bake in a preheated 350° oven until the juices run clear when the pâté is pierced with a fork, 1 to 1¼ hours. Let stand to cool; refrigerate. Serve sliced, accompanied with crusty bread.

6 to 8 servings

Salmon Mousse

½ cup water
2 envelopes
  unflavored gelatin
1 can (7 oz) red
  salmon,
  undrained
Juice of ½ lemon
⅔ cup sour cream
Salt and pepper
½ cup heavy cream,
  lightly whipped
1 cucumber, peeled,
  seeded and
  chopped

Place 3 tablespoons of the water in a small saucepan; sprinkle in the gelatin. Let stand 5 minutes. Heat over low heat until dissolved.

Place the gelatin mixture, salmon with its juice, lemon juice, sour cream and remaining water in a blender and puree. Transfer to a bowl and season to taste with salt and pepper; refrigerate until just beginning to set. Fold in the whipped cream and cucumber.

Spoon into an oiled 1-quart mold. Refrigerate until set. Unmold onto a serving dish; garnish with cucumber slices or dill. Serve with buttered pumpernickel bread.

About 3 cups

Avocado Mousse

2 avocados, cut up
⅔ cup plain yogurt
½ cup milk
2 envelopes
    unflavored gelatin
2 tablespoons cold
    water
½ cup boiling water
1 teaspoon finely
    chopped onion
1 teaspoon lemon
    juice
1 teaspoon
    Worcestershire
    sauce
Salt and pepper
½ cup heavy cream,
    whipped

Place the avocados in a blender with the yogurt and milk. Soak the gelatin in 2 tablespoons cold water to soften; pour boiling water over and stir until dissolved. Add the gelatin mixture, onion, lemon juice and Worcestershire to the avocados in the blender and puree.

Transfer to a bowl and season to taste with salt and pepper; refrigerate until just beginning to thicken. Fold in whipped cream. Pour into an oiled 5-cup mold. Refrigerate until set. Unmold onto a serving dish. Garnish with watercress if desired.
About 4 cups

Cheddar-Shrimp Mousse

2 eggs, separated
1 cup grated sharp
  Cheddar cheese
1 tablespoon grated
  Parmesan cheese
2 teaspoons prepared
  hot mustard
Cayenne pepper
Grated nutmeg
Salt
1¼ cups heavy
  cream, whipped
4 cooked shrimp,
  chopped

Beat the egg yolks until pale yellow, stir in the cheeses, mustard and cayenne, nutmeg and salt to taste.

Fold the cream into the cheese mixture with the shrimp.

Beat the egg whites until stiff peaks form; fold into the cheese mixture.

Spoon the mousse into small ramekins or serving dishes; refrigerate until serving time.

Serve with a shrimp garnish if desired.

4 to 6 servings

Asparagus and Crab Mousse

1 can (12 oz)
  asparagus
1 can (6 oz) crabmeat
½ cup (about)
  chicken broth
2 tablespoons butter
3 tablespoons flour
2 envelopes
  unflavored gelatin
3 tablespoons dry
  white wine
1 cup mayonnaise
½ cup heavy cream,
  whipped

Drain and reserve the liquid from the asparagus and crabmeat, adding enough chicken broth to make 1 cup.

Melt the butter in a medium saucepan over medium heat. Stir in the flour; cook 1 minute. Stir in 1 cup broth mixture; heat to boiling. Reduce heat; simmer, stirring constantly, 2 minutes. Coarsely chop the asparagus and flake the crabmeat. Stir into the sauce.

Dissolve the gelatin in wine over low heat; stir into the asparagus mixture. Fold in the mayonnaise and the cream. Spoon the mixture into a lightly oiled 1-quart mold. Refrigerate until set.

Unmold onto a serving dish and garnish with dill if desired.

6 to 8 servings

Smoked Trout Mousse

3 smoked trout
1 cup dry white wine
2 teaspoons finely
   chopped onion
½ clove garlic,
   crushed
1 parsley sprig
1 teaspoon dried
   tarragon
¼ teaspoon dried
   thyme
2 bay leaves
Salt and pepper
1¼ cups sour cream

Place the trout in a saucepan with the wine, onion, garlic, herbs and salt and pepper to taste. Cover and simmer 10 minutes. Lift fish from pan, reserving the cooking liquid. Skin and bone the fish and place chunks of fish in a blender container.

Boil the cooking liquid until it is reduced by one-third; strain into the blender. Puree the fish and turn out into a bowl; fold in the sour cream. Cover and refrigerate. To serve, spoon into dishes. Garnish with lemon or lime slices if desired.

6 servings

93

INDEX